passion

our love is loud

:: music from the passion experience tour ::

	Full Version	Chord Sheets
Come Thou Fount of Every Blessing	2	58
Dance in the River	4	59
Enough	6	60
Famous One	10	61
*Forever	13	62
God of Wonders	16	63
*God of Wrath	20	64
Here I Am to Worship	24	65
Madly	27	66
My Glorious	32	67
Our Love is Loud	44	68
Prepare the Way	36	70
Psalm 126	40	71
*Savior of the World	49	72
Sweep Me Away	52	73
Wonderful King	54	74

*bonus song

©2002 worshiptogether®
P.O. Box 5085, Brentwood, TN 37024-5085
All rights reserved.
e-mail: productinfo@worshiptogether.com

Come, Thou Fount of Every Blessing

Traditional
Arranged by David Crowder

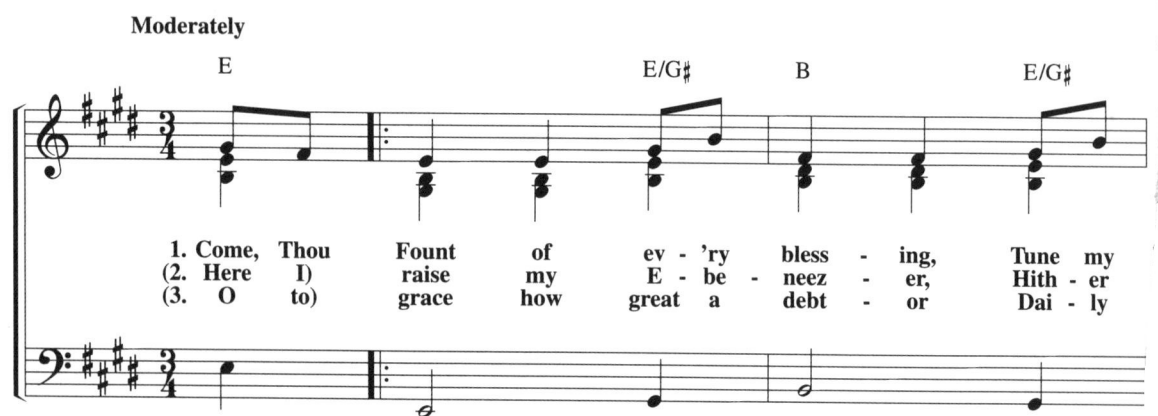

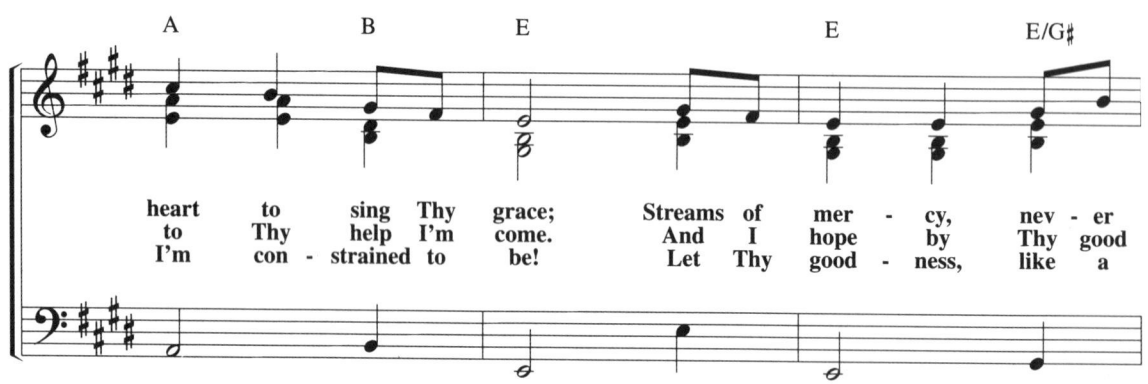

Arrangement Copyright © 2002 worshiptogether.com songs/Six Steps Music.
Administered by EMI Christian Music Publishing, P.O. Box 5085, Brentwood, TN 37204-5085.
All rights reserved. Used by permission.

Dance in the River

**Words and Music by
MARTIN SMITH**

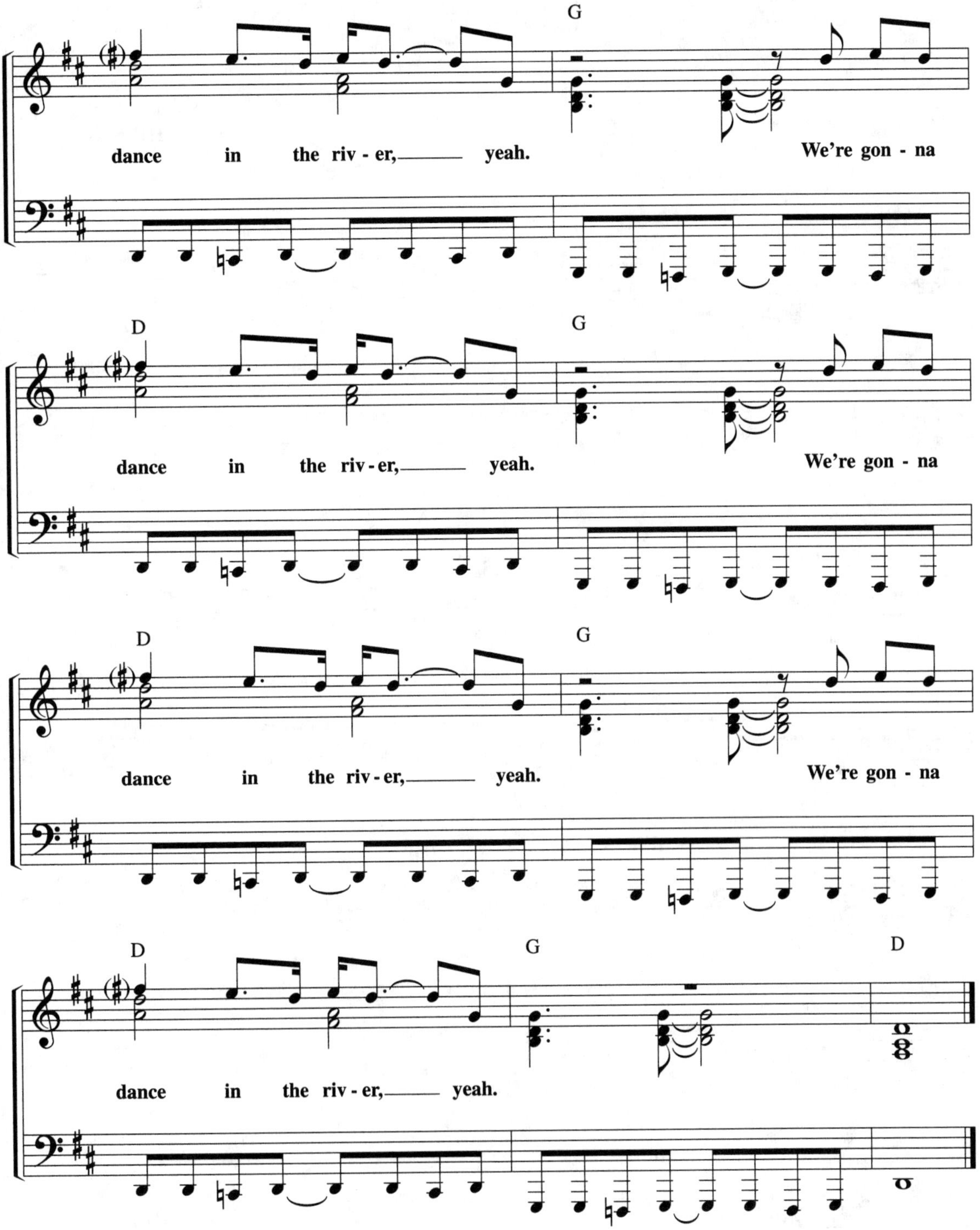

G
dance in the riv - er, yeah.
We're gon - na
D
G
dance in the riv - er, yeah.
We're gon - na
D
G
dance in the riv - er, yeah.
We're gon - na
D
G
D
dance in the riv - er, yeah.

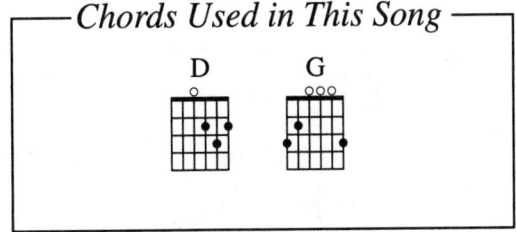

Chords Used in This Song

D
G

6

Enough

Words and Music by
CHRIS TOMLIN
and LOUIE GIGLIO

Copyright © 2002 worshiptogether.com songs/Six Steps Music.
Administered by EMI Christian Music Publishing, P.O. Box 5085, Brentwood, TN 37204-5085.
All rights reserved. Used by permission.

E♭sus (Dsus)
A♭/C (G/B)
D♭2 (C2)
worth living for; still more awe-
You are ev'ry-thing; still more awe-
1.
B♭m7 (Am7)
E♭sus (Dsus)
-some than I know. And all of You
2.
B♭m7 (Am7)
E♭sus (Dsus)
-some than I know.
A♭ (G)
D♭2 (C2)
E♭sus (Dsus)
D♭2 (C2)
More than all I want, more than all I need,
A♭/C (G/B)
D♭2 (C2)
E♭sus (Dsus)
yeah. You are more than e-nough for me.
A♭ (G)
D♭2 (C2)
E♭sus (Dsus)
D♭2 (C2)
More than all I know, more than all I'm can

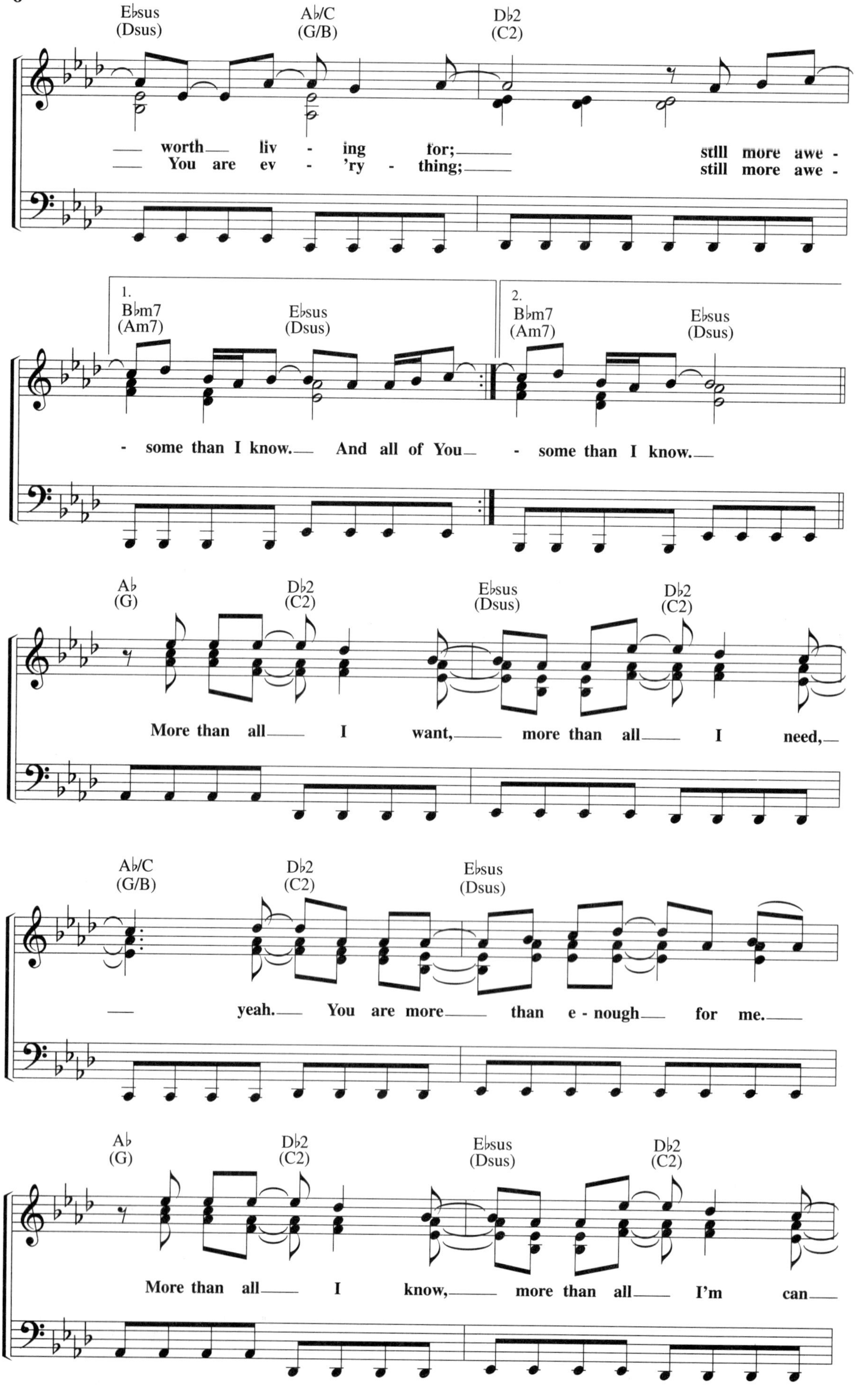

D.S. al CODA
A♭/C
(G/B)
D♭2
(C2)
E♭sus
(Dsus)
see, You are more than e - nough. And all of You

CODA
E♭sus
(Dsus)
A♭
(G)
is more than e - nough.

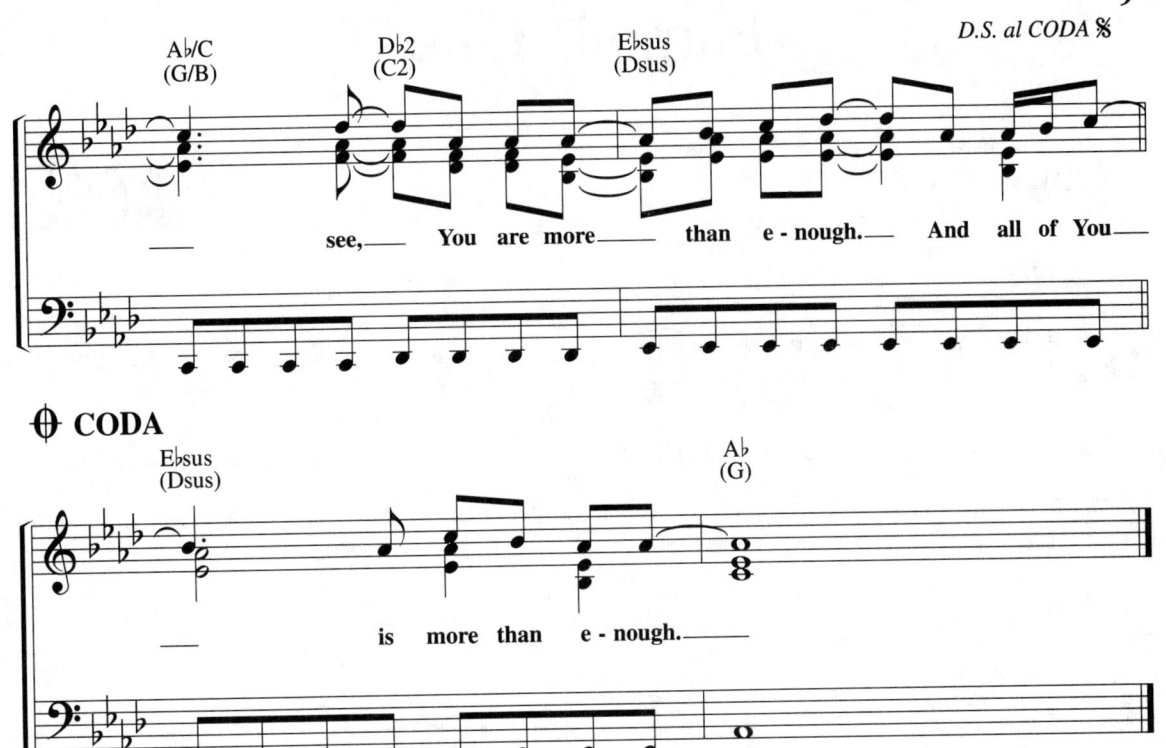

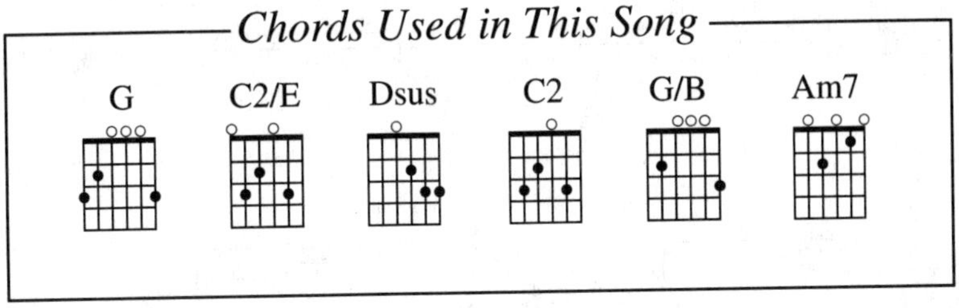
Chords Used in This Song
G
C2/E
Dsus
C2
G/B
Am7

Famous One

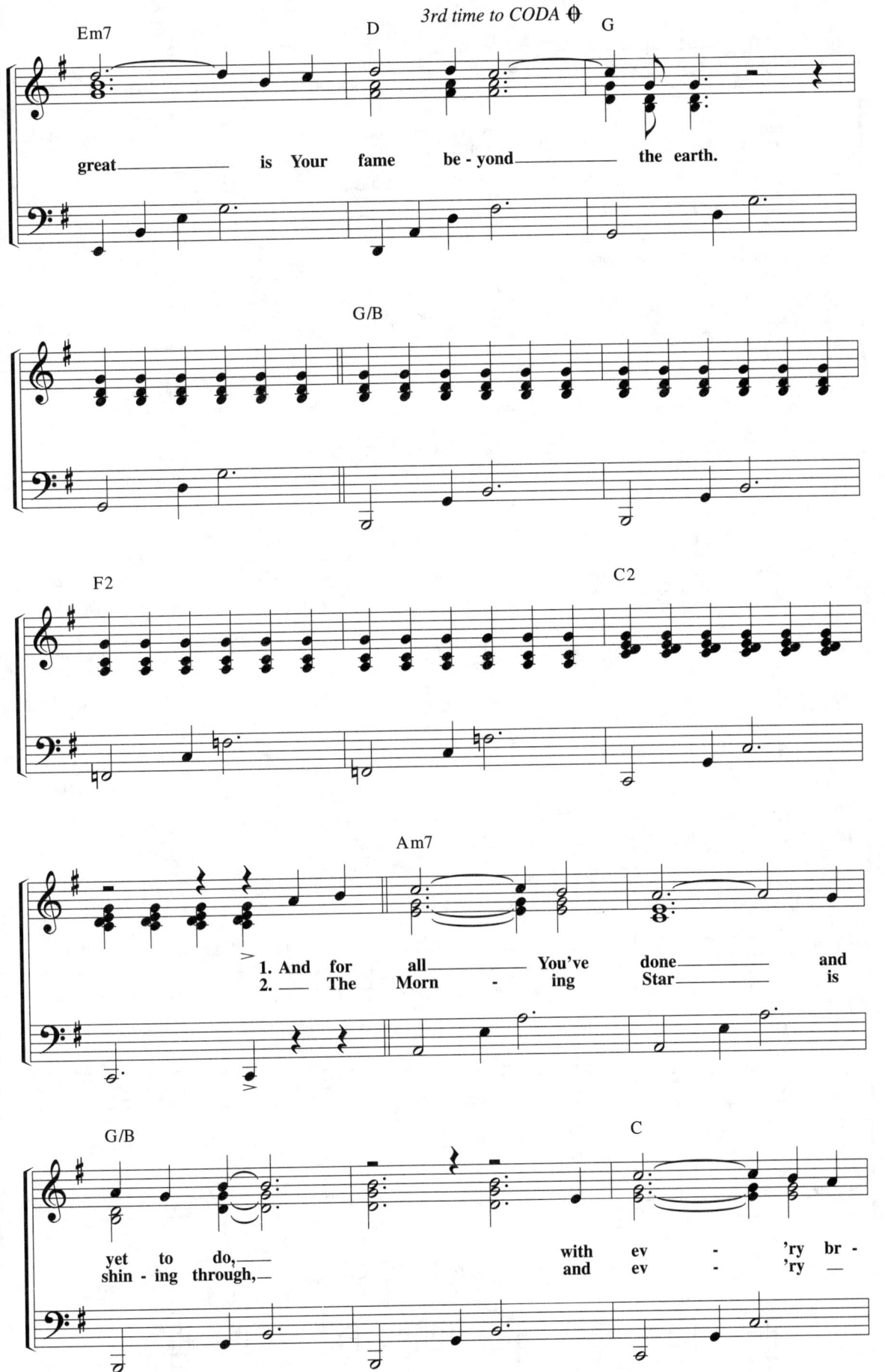

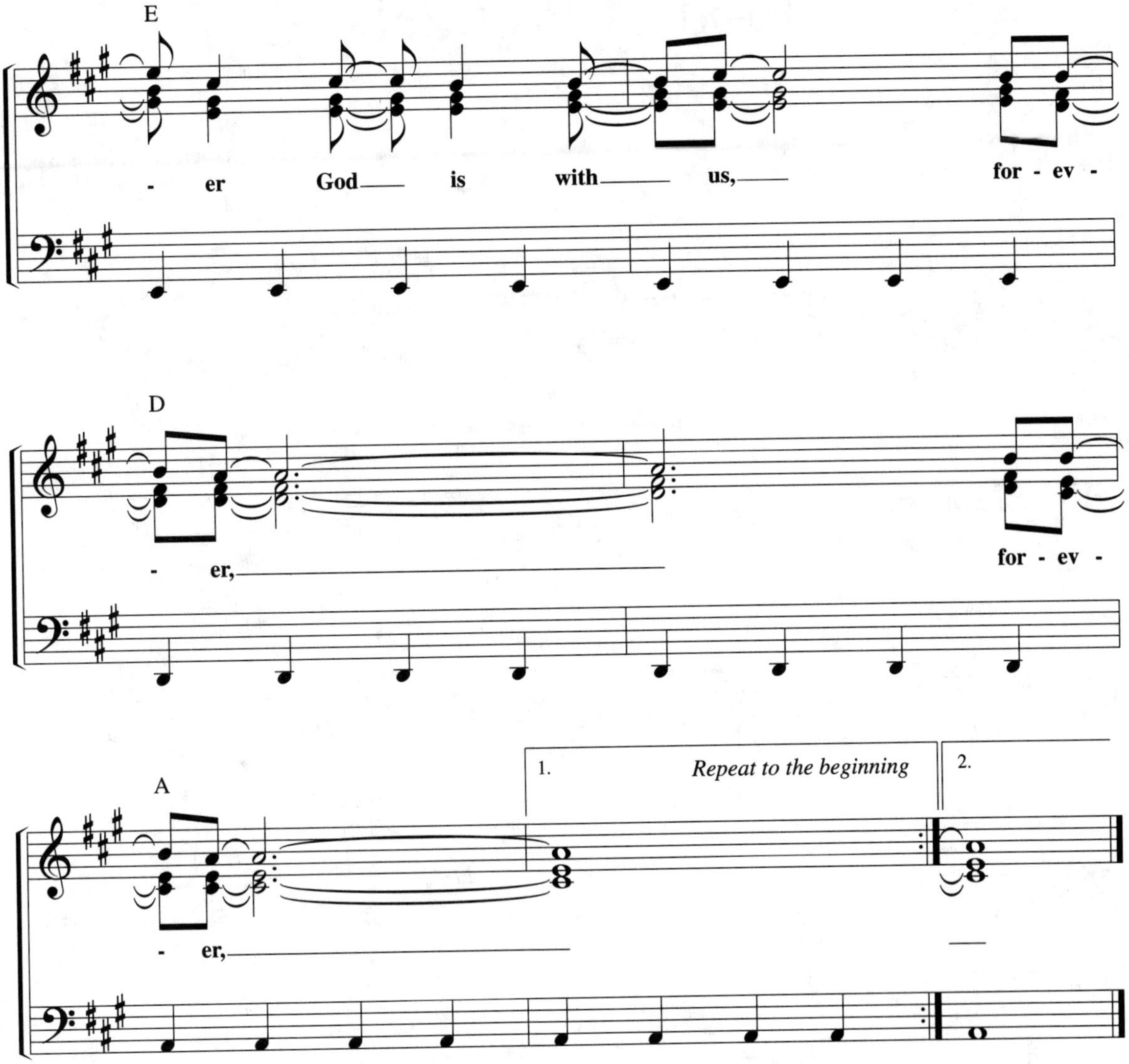

E
- er God is with us, for - ev -
D
- er, for - ev -
A
1. Repeat to the beginning
2.
- er,

Chords Used in This Song
A
D
E
D2/F♯
F♯m7

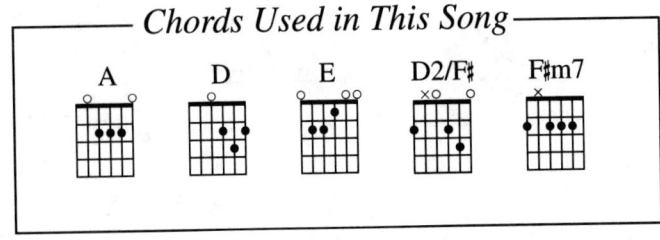

God of Wrath

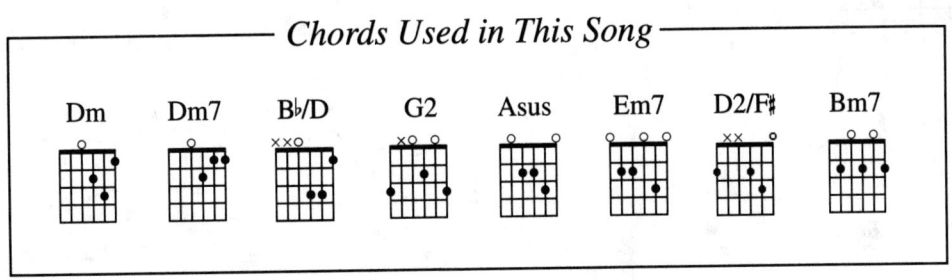

Chords Used in This Song

Dm Dm7 B♭/D G2 Asus Em7 D2/F♯ Bm7

23

Here I Am to Worship

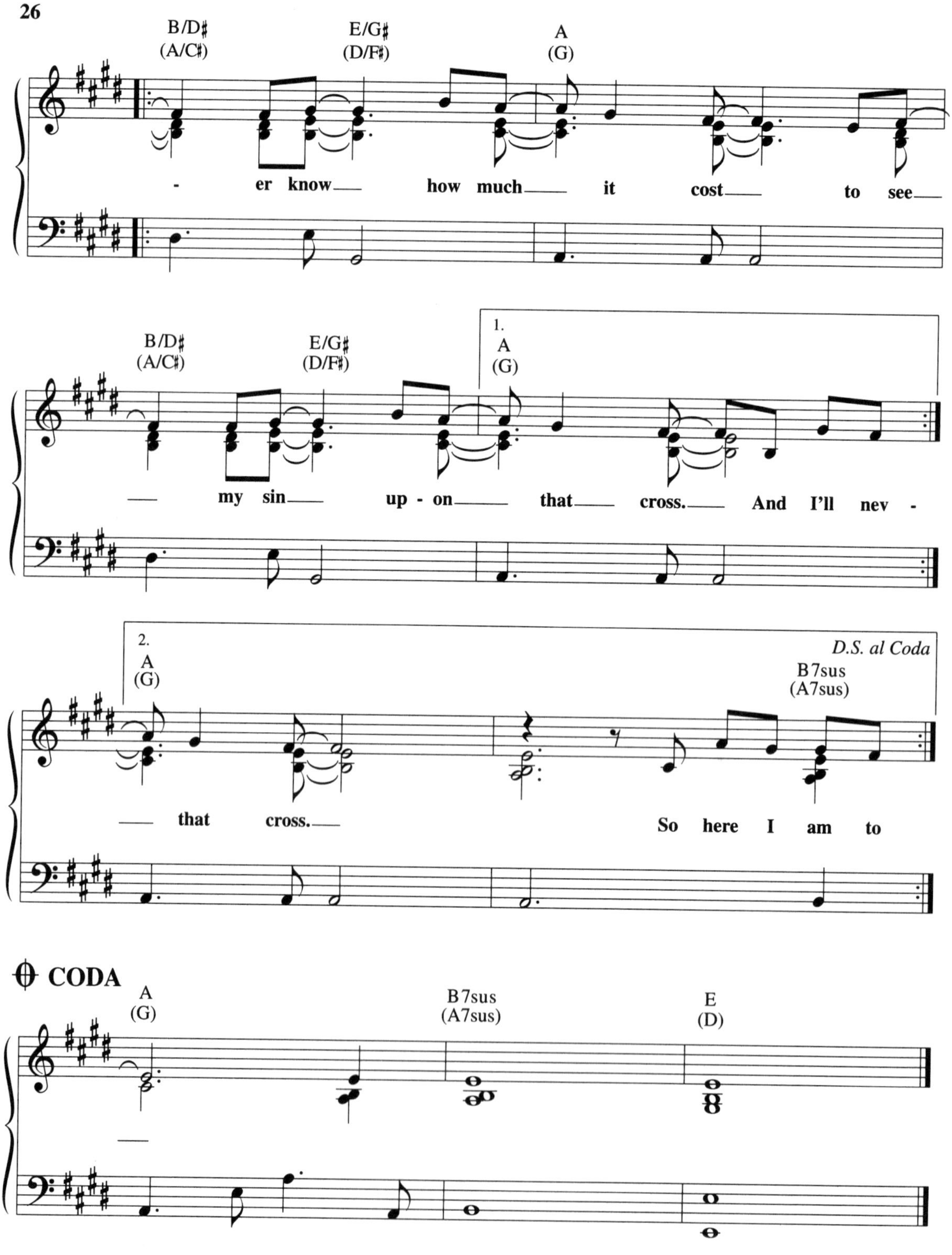

B/D♯
(A/C♯)
E/G♯
(D/F♯)
A
(G)
- er know how much it cost to see
my sin up - on that cross. And I'll nev -
1.
2.
that cross.
D.S. al Coda
B7sus
(A7sus)
So here I am to
CODA
E
(D)

Chords Used in This Song
D
Asus
Em
D/G
A7sus
A/C♯
D/F♯
G

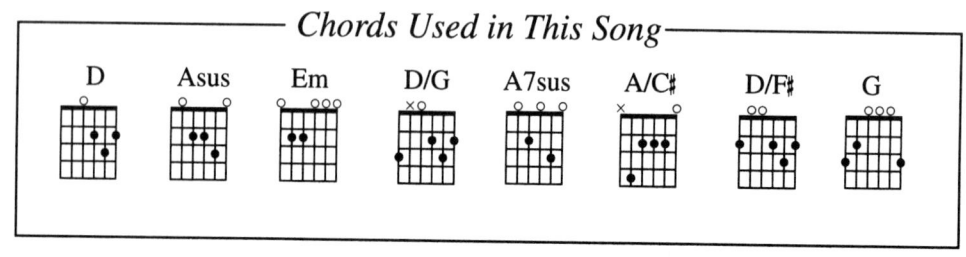

Madly

27

Words and Music by
STEVE FEE

Copyright © 2002 worshiptogether.com songs/Six Steps Music.
Administered by EMI Christian Music Publishing, P.O. Box 5085, Brentwood, TN 37204-5085.
All rights reserved. Used by permission.

My Glorious

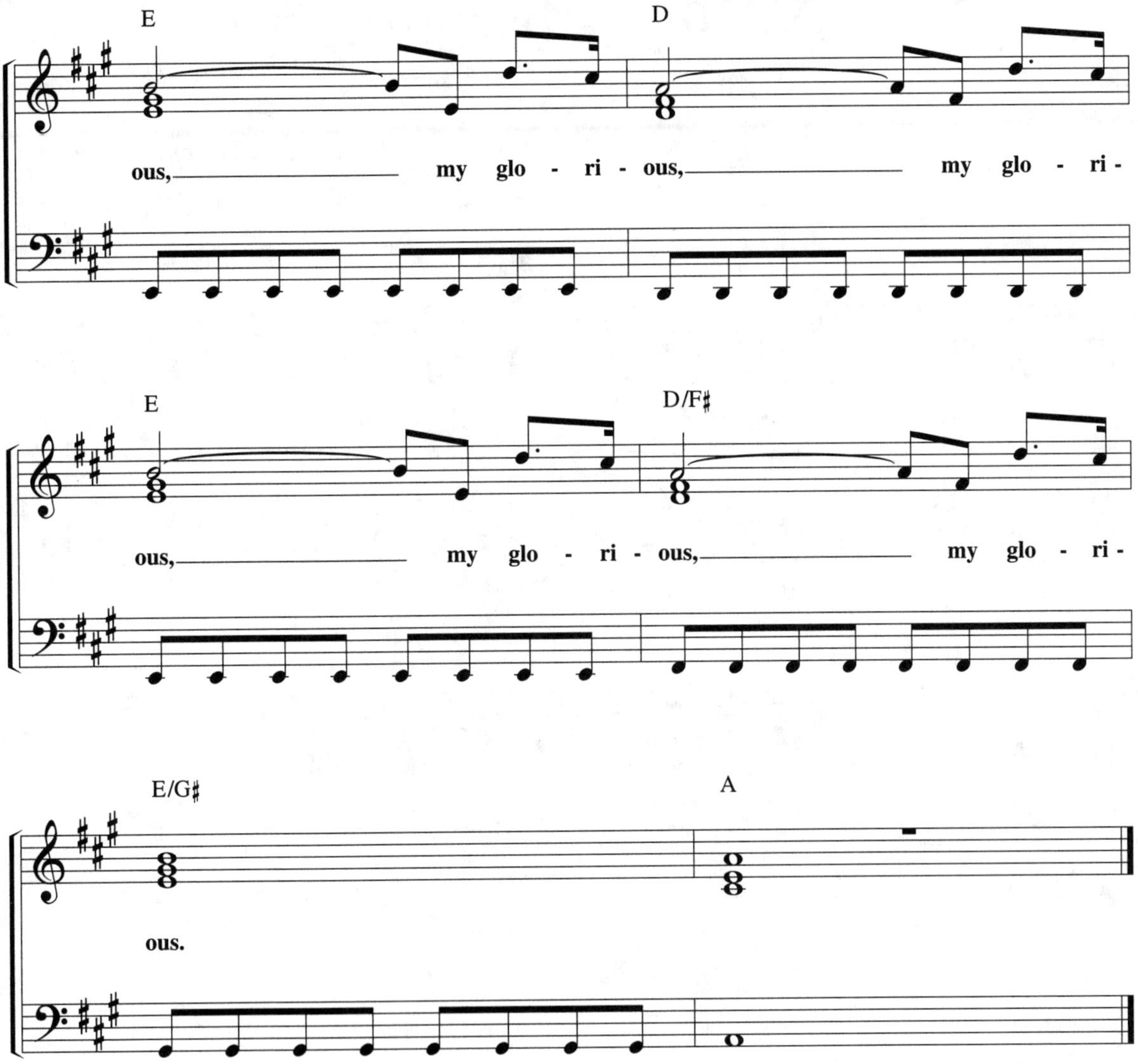
E
D
ous, my glo - ri - ous, my glo - ri -
E
D/F♯
ous, my glo - ri - ous, my glo - ri -
E/G♯
A
ous.

Chords Used in This Song

F♯m7
D
Bm
A/C♯
Bsus
A
E/G♯
E
Bm7
C♯m7
4fr
D/F♯

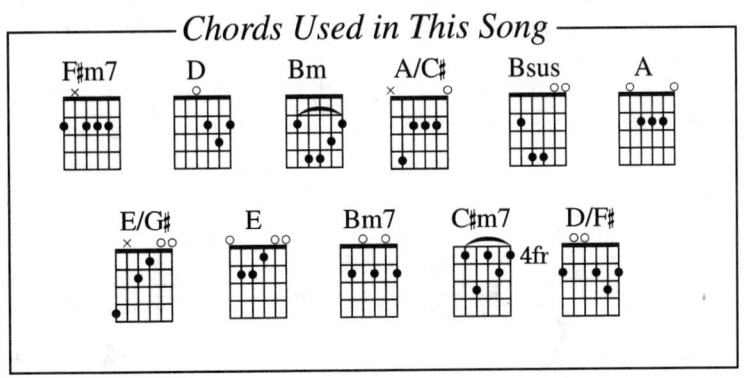

Prepare the Way

**Words and Music by
CHARLIE HALL
and LOUIE GIGLIO**

Copyright © 2002 worshiptogether.com songs/Six Steps Music.
Administered by EMI Christian Music Publishing, P.O. Box 5085, Brentwood, TN 37204-5085.
All rights reserved. Used by permission.

D
Bm
D/F♯
Je - sus, Je - sus, Je - sus, Je -
G2
D
Bm
2nd time to CODA
- sus. Je - sus, Je - sus,
D/F♯
G2
Je - sus, Je - sus.
D
Bm
1. You are the Light of the world, You are the Light of the world,
2. You are the King of the earth, You are the King of the earth,
D/F♯
G2
You are the Light of the world, Je - sus.
You are the King of the earth, Je - sus.

| D | Bm |

You are the Light of the world, You are the Light of the world,
You are the King of the earth, You are the King of the earth,

D/F# G2 *1.*

You are the Light of the world, Je - sus.
You are the King of the earth, Je -

2. G2   D   Bm

- sus.   Je-sus,   Je-sus,   Je-sus,   Je-sus,   Je-sus,

D/F#   G2

Je-sus,   Je-sus.   Je-sus,

D   Bm

Je-sus,   Je-sus,   Je-sus,   Je-sus,

39

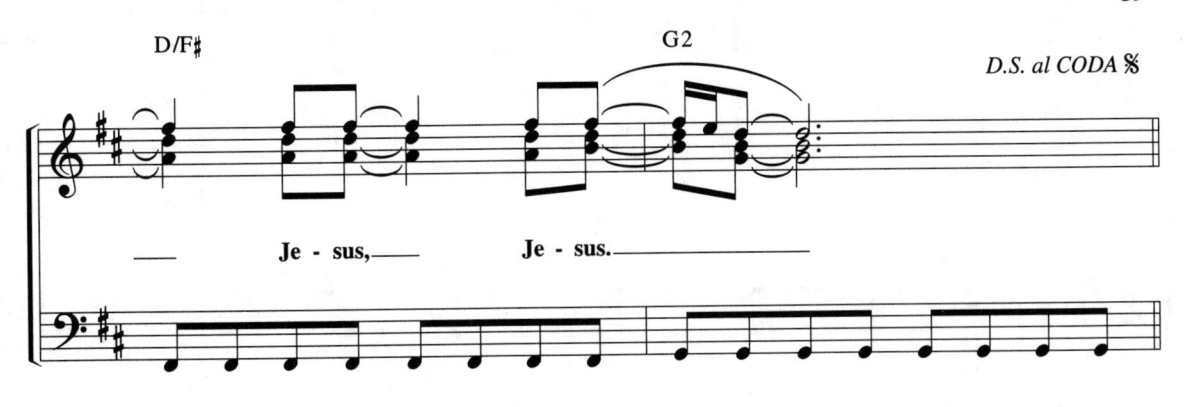

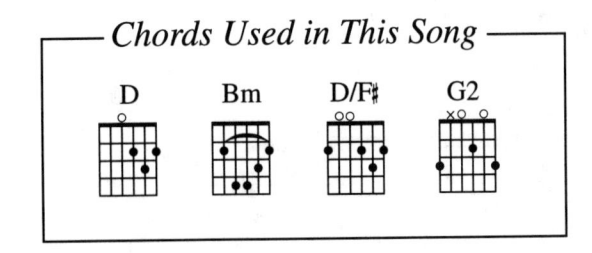

Psalm 126

With joy

Words and Music by
CHARLIE HALL

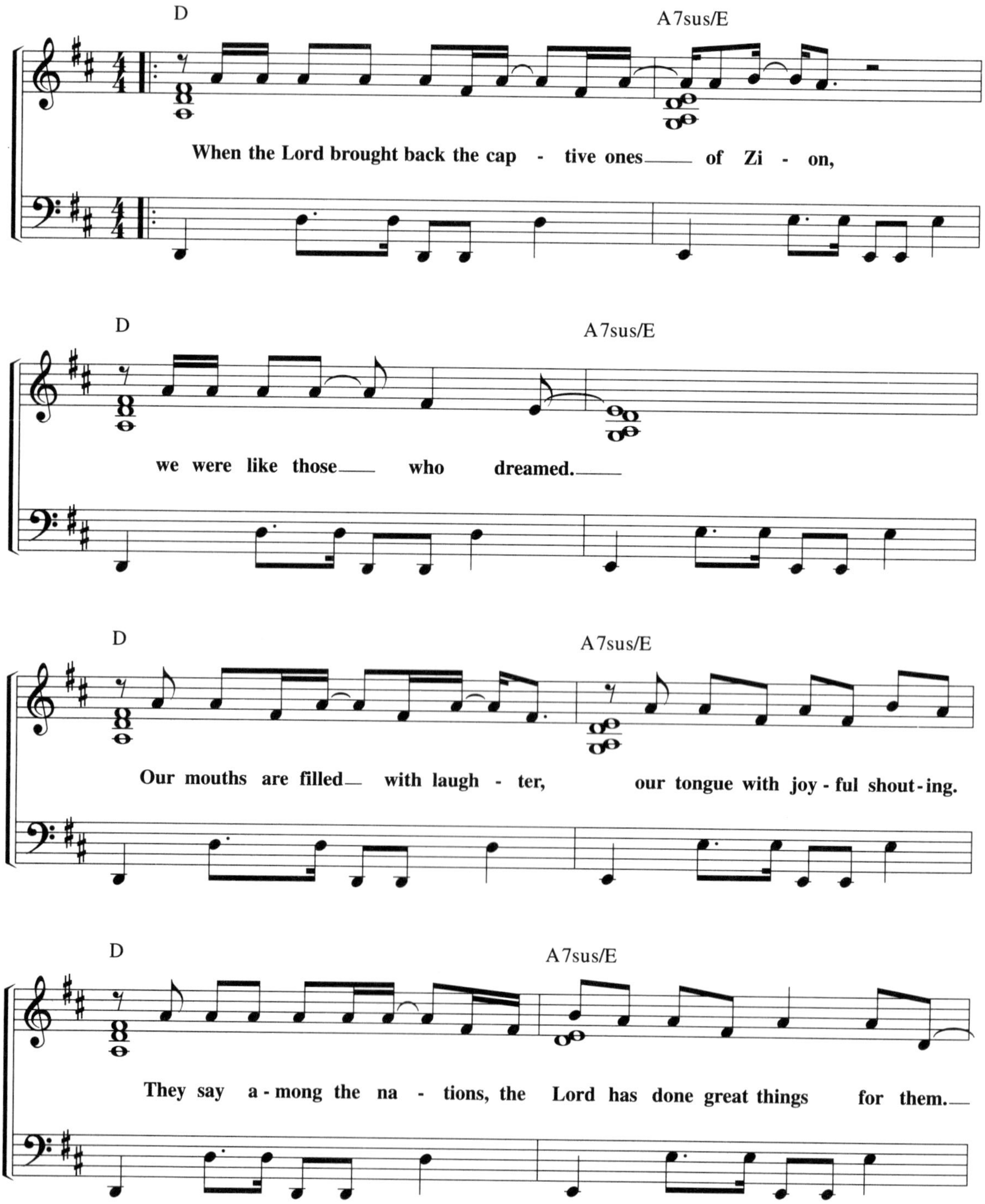

41

have done great things, yeah, You

have done great things, Father, You

have done great things. You've re-stored

our hearts; like streams, they flow. Those

who sowed in tears have reaped their joy,

43

Our Love Is Loud

Words and Music by
DAVID CROWDER

Joyfully

1. When we sing, _____ hear _____ our songs _____
(2. When we sing) _____ loud, hear _____ our songs _____
to You; _____ when we dance, _____
to You; _____ when we dance _____ 'round,
feel _____ us move _____ to You; _____ when we laugh,
feel _____ us move _____ to You; _____ when we laugh _____
a-loud, fill _____ our smiles _____ with You.
fill _____ our smiles _____ with You.

Copyright © 2002 worshiptogether.com songs/Six Steps Music.
Administered by EMI Christian Music Publishing, P.O. Box 5085, Brentwood, TN 37204-5085.
All rights reserved. Used by permission.

A2
E
F♯m7
When we lift our voic - es loud - er still, can
C♯m7
A2
E
You hear us? Can You feel? We love You, Lord, we love
E/D♯
C♯m7
A2
You, we love You.
We love
E
E/D♯
You, Lord, we love You, we love You.
3rd time to CODA
C♯m7
1.
A2
E

E/D♯
C♯m7
A2
2. When we sing
2.
A2
E
F♯m7
And our love is big, our love is loud. Fill
E/G♯
A2
this place with this love, now. And our love
E
F♯m7
is big, our love is loud. Fill
E/G♯
A2
this place with this love, now. And our love

47

-er still. Our God is near, our God

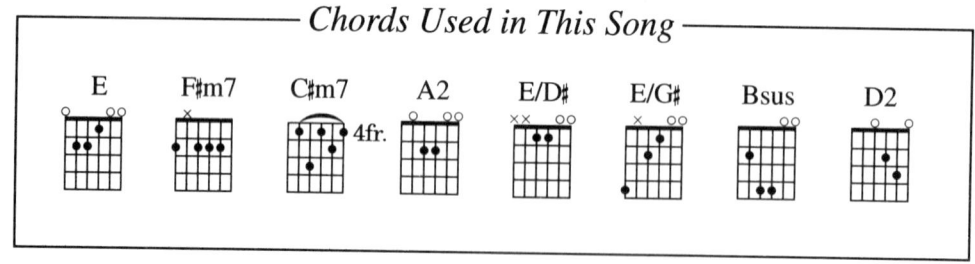

1.
A2
is here. We lift

2.
A2
is here.

E

Chords Used in This Song

E F#m7 C#m7 A2 E/D# E/G# Bsus D2

Savior of the World

Words and Music by
CHARLIE HALL

With emotion

_____ will run _____ in - to _____ the Fa - ther's arms. _____ They _____ sing: Oh Je - sus, lift - ed up _____ on high, _____ cru - ci - fied _____ for fall - en man, You died and then _____ You rose _____ a - gain, _____ oh Je - sus, Sav - ior of _____ the world. You've beat - en death _____ and giv - en life, You came to set _____ the pris - 'ner free, You died 'cause You're _____ in love _____ with me,

51

1. F♯m7   **2.** F♯m7   E

Oh Je-sus, Sav-ior of the world. Sav-ior of the world.

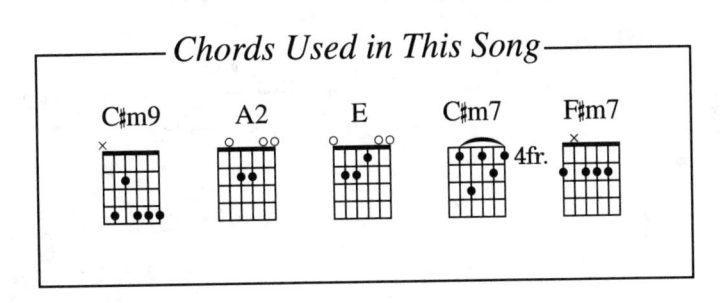

---Chords Used in This Song---

C♯m9   A2   E   C♯m7 (4fr.)   F♯m7

Sweep Me Away

**Words and Music by
CHARLIE HALL, KENDALL COMBS, WILL HUNT,
BRIAN BERGMAN and TODD CROMWELL**

Slowly, with much emotion

1. Sud-den-ly I feel You hold-ing me,
2. Sud-den-ly I feel Your hand in mine,
3. Sud-den-ly I feel You lead-ing me,
4. Sud-den-ly I feel Your heart in mine,

sud-den-ly I feel You hold-ing me,
sud-den-ly I feel Your hand in mine,
sud-den-ly I feel You lead-ing me,
sud-den-ly I feel Your heart in mine,

sud-den-ly I feel You hold-ing me,
sud-den-ly I feel Your hand in mine,
sud-den-ly I feel You lead-ing me,
sud-den-ly I feel Your heart in mine,

Copyright © 2002 worshiptogether.com songs/Six Steps Music.
Administered by EMI Christian Music Publishing, P.O. Box 5085, Brentwood, TN 37204-5085.
All rights reserved. Used by permission.

sud-den-ly I feel__ You hold-ing me.
sud-den-ly I feel__ Your hand__ in mine.
sud-den-ly I feel__ You lead-ing me.
sud-den-ly I feel__ Your heart__ in mine.

Sweep me a-way, sweep me a-way, sweep me a-way, sweep me a-way.

Chords Used in This Song

B   Bsus   A/B   B2

Wonderful King

Words and Music by
DAVID CROWDER

With adoration

55

56

57

A2 | Bsus

here. Oh, won-der-ful sound,—— love our heav-en now.——

A/C# | B/D#

Oh, beau-ti-ful sound,—— the joy of heav-en

A2 | Bsus | *D.S. al CODA*

here. Oh, won-der-ful sound,—— love our heav-en now.——

CODA

A2

King.——

— Chords Used in This Song —

E   E/G#   A2   F#m7   Bsus   B/D#

Come, Thou Fount of Every Blessing

Traditional, Arranged by DAVID CROWDER

E   E/G#   B   A

VERSE 1:

```
E            E/G# B     E/G# A  B    E
```
Come, Thou Fount of ev'ry blessing, Tune my heart to sing Thy grace

```
           E     E/G# B     E/G# A  B    E
```
Streams of mercy, never ceasing, Call for songs of loudest praise

Teach me some melodious sonnet Sung by flaming tongues above

```
           E/G# B    E/G#  A      B      E  E/G# B E/G# A B E
```
Praise the mount; I'm fixed upon it, Mount of God's redeeming love

VERSE 2:

```
E           E/G# B    E/G# A   B    E
```
Here I raise my Ebe-neezer, Hither to Thy help I'm come

```
    E      E/G#    B     E/G# A  B    E
```
And I hope by Thy good pleasure Safely to arrive at home.

Jesus sought me when a stranger Wand'ring from the fold of God

```
            E/G#   B     E/G# A     B      E  E/G# B E/G# A B E
```
He, to rescue me from danger   Interposed His precious blood

VERSE 3:

```
E          E/G# B    E/G# A   B     E
```
O to grace how great a debtor Daily I'm constrained to be!

```
    E      E/G# B    E/G#  A   B     E
```
Let Thy goodness, like a fetter Bind my wand'ring heart to Thee

Prone to wander, Lord, I feel it; Prone to leave the God I love

```
            E/G#    B    E/G# A    B      E  E/G# B E/G# A B E
```
Here's my heart, O take and seal it, Seal it for Thy courts above

Arrangement © 2002 worshiptogether.com songs / Six Steps Music. Administered by EMI Christian Music Publishing.
P.O. Box 5085, Brentwood, TN 37204-5085. All rights reserved. Used by permission.

Dance in the River

MARTIN SMITH

     D
We're gonna dance in the river, yeah

We're gonna dance in the river, yeah

We're gonna dance in the river, yeah

We're gonna dance in the river, yeah

                         G
We're gonna dance in the river, yeah
    D   **G**
We're gonna dance in the river, yeah
    D   **G**
We're gonna dance in the river, yeah
    D   **G D**
We're gonna dance in the river, yeah

© 2002 Curious? Music UK. All rights in the US and Canada administered by EMI Christian Music Publishing.
P.O. Box 5085, Brentwood, TN 37204-5085. All rights reserved. Used by permission.

Enough

CHRIS TOMLIN and LOUIE GIGLIO

Chords: G   C2/E   Dsus   C2   G/B   Am7

Capo 1 (G)

CHORUS:

```
        G        C2/E          Dsus     C2      G   C2/E        Dsus
All of You is more than enough     for  all of me, for   ev'ry thirst
        C2       G    C2/E       Dsus     C2              G/B
And    ev'ry need. You       satisfy    me    with Your love
        C2            Dsus              G   (C2/E Dsus C2 G C2/E Dsus C2)
And all I have in You      is more than enough
```

VERSE 1:

```
G          C2       Dsus       G/B     C2
 You're my  supply,   my breath    of life
           Am7             Dsus
Still more awesome than I know
G          C2       Dsus       G/B     C2
 You're my  reward,    worth living for
           Am7             Dsus
Still more awesome than I know
```

(REPEAT CHORUS)

VERSE 2:

```
G          C2       Dsus          G/B     C2
 You're my sacrifice of greatest price
           Am7             Dsus
Still more awesome than I know
G          C2       Dsus          G/B     C2
 You're my coming King,  You are ev'rything
           Am7             Dsus
Still more awesome than I know
```

BRIDGE:

```
G            C2          Dsus           C2         G/B
 More than all   I want,    more than all   I need,   yeah
C2       Dsus
 You are more than enough for me
G            C2          Dsus           C2         G/B
 More than all   I know,    more than all   I can    see
C2       Dsus
 You are more than enough
```

(REPEAT CHORUS)

© 2002 worshiptogether.com songs / Six Steps Music. Administered by EMI Christian Music Publishing.
P.O. Box 5085, Brentwood, TN 37204-5085. All rights reserved. Used by permission.

Famous One

CHRIS TOMLIN and JESSE REEVES

CHORUS:

G   G/B   C2
You are the Lord,   the famous One, famous One
Em7   D   C
Great is Your name in all   the earth
   G   G/B   C2
The heavens declare   You're glorious, glorious
Em7   D   G   G/B F2 C2
Great is Your fame beyond   the earth

VERSE 1:

     Am7   G/B
And for all You've done and yet to do
   C   G
With ev'ry breath, I'm   praising You
     Am7   G/B
Desire of nations and   ev'ry heart
   C
You alone are God
   Dsus
You alone are God

(REPEAT CHORUS)

VERSE 2:

     Am7   G/B
The Morning Star is shining through
   C   G
And ev'ry eye is   watching You
     Am7   G/B
Reveal Thy nature and   miracles
     C
You are   beautiful
     Dsus
You are beautiful

(REPEAT CHORUS)

© 2002 worshiptogether.com songs / Six Steps Music. Administered by EMI Christian Music Publishing.
P.O. Box 5085, Brentwood, TN 37204-5085. All rights reserved. Used by permission.

Forever

CHRIS TOMLIN

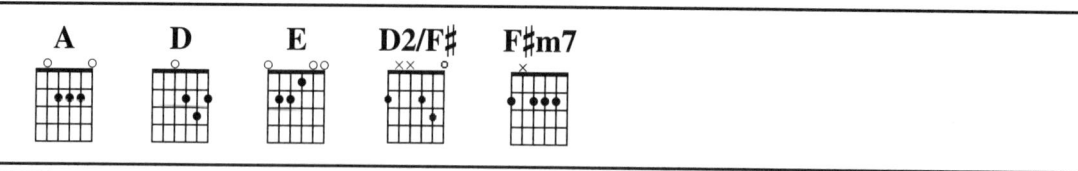

Chords: A · D · E · D2/F# · F#m7

VERSE 1:

     A
Give thanks to the Lord our God and King
His love endures forever

D
For He is good, He is above all things
               A
His love endures forever
    E   D/F#
Sing praise, sing praise

VERSE 2:

A
  With a mighty hand and outstretched arm
His love endures forever

D
  For the life that's been reborn
               A
His love endures forever
    E   D/F#   E   D/F#
Sing praise, sing praise, sing praise, sing praise

CHANNEL:

    A   F#m7
Forever God is faithful, forever God is strong
   E   D   A
Forever God is with us, forever, forever

VERSE 3:

A
  From the rising to the setting sun
His love endures forever
        D
And by the grace of God we will carry on
              A
His love endures forever
    E   D/F#   E   D/F#
Sing praise, sing praise, sing praise, sing praise

(REPEAT CHANNEL)

© 2001 worshiptogether.com songs / Six Steps Music. Administered by EMI Christian Music Publishing.
P.O. Box 5085, Brentwood, TN 37204-5085. All rights reserved. Used by permission.

God of Wonders

MARC BYRD and STEVE HINDALONG

Capo 1 (G)

VERSE 1:

Dsus   Em   C2
   Lord of all   creation

Dsus   Em   C2
   Of water, earth   and   sky

Dsus   Em   C2
   The heavens are Your tabernacle

Dsus   Em   C2
   Glory to the Lord   on   high

CHORUS:

G   D
God of wonders beyond our galaxy

     Am7 C2   G   D
You are holy, holy; the universe declares Your majesty

     Am7 C2
You are holy, holy; Lord of heaven and earth

                      (Dsus Em C2 Dsus Em C2)
Lord of heaven and earth

VERSE 2:

Dsus   Em   C2
   Early in   the morning

Dsus   Em   C2
   I will celebrate   the   light

Dsus   Em   C2
   And as I stumble in the darkness

Dsus   Em   C2
   I will call Your name   by   night

(REPEAT CHORUS)

TAG:

Am7   C2
   Hallelujah! to the Lord of heaven and earth

Am7   C2
   Hallelujah! to the Lord of heaven and earth

Am7   C2   G
   Hallelujah! to the Lord of heaven and earth

© 2000 Storm Boy Music / New Spring Publishing / Never Say Never Songs. All rights reserved. Used by permission.

God of Wrath

DAVID CROWDER

Chords: Dm, Dm7, Bb/D, G2, Asus, Em7, D2/F#, Bm7

Capo 1 (F, D)

VERSE 1:

Dm Dm7	Bb/D Dm7
God of wrath, God of love

| Dm Dm7 | Bb/D Dm7 |
God of earth and God above

| Dm Dm7 | Bb/D Dm7 |
God of hope, God of peace

| Dm Dm7 | Bb/D Dm7 | Dm Dm7 Bb/D Dm7 |
God of you and God of me

VERSE 2:

| Dm Dm7 | Bb/D Dm7 |
God of day, God of night

| Dm Dm7 | Bb/D Dm7 |
God the just and God the light

| Dm Dm7 | Bb/D Dm7 |
God of the strong, God of the weak

| Dm Dm7 | Bb/D Dm7 G2 |
God of you and God of me

BRIDGE:

    Asus   Em7   D2/F# Bm7   G2
My love for You, my heart for You, my life for You, all I am for You

    Asus   Em7   D2/F# Bm7   G2 (Asus) *1st time*
My love for You, my heart for You, my life for You, all I am for You

(REPEAT VERSES 1, 2 & BRIDGE)

TAG:

G2   **Asus**
Blood through my veins for You; I give my world to You

Em7   **D2/F#**   **Bm7**
All I am and all I have, I lay it down for You

G2   **Asus**
Dancing 'round with You, spinning 'round with You

Em7   **D2/F#**   **Bm7**   **G2**
Laughing loud with You, my love, my love

© 2002 worshiptogether.com songs / Six Steps Music. Administered by EMI Christian Music Publishing.
P.O. Box 5085, Brentwood, TN 37204-5085. All rights reserved. Used by permission.

Here I Am to Worship
TIM HUGHES

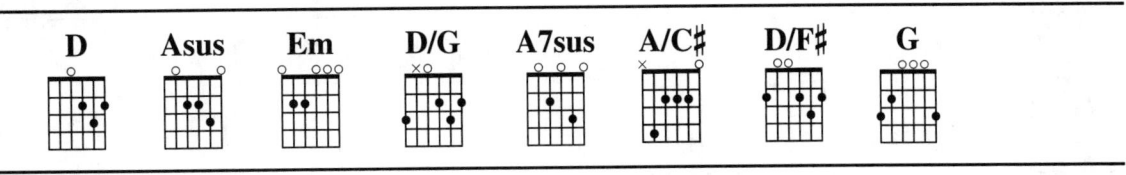

D   Asus   Em   D/G   A7sus   A/C#   D/F#   G

Capo 2 (D)

VERSE 1:

D   Asus   Em
Light of the World, You stepped down into darkness

D   Asus   D/G
Opened my eyes, let me   see

D   Asus   Em
Beauty that made this heart adore You

D   Asus   D/G
Hope of a life spent with   You

CHORUS:

           A7sus D   A/C#
So here I am to worship, here I am to bow down

           D/F#   G
Here I am to say that You're my God

                     D   A/C#
And You're altogether lovely, altogether worthy

        D/F#   G (A7sus) *1st time*
Altogether wonderful to me

VERSE 2:

D   Asus   Em
King of all days, oh so highly exalted

D   Asus   D/G
Glorious in heaven above

D   Asus   Em
Humbly You came to the Earth You created

D   Asus   D/G
All for love's sake became   poor

BRIDGE:

     A/C#   D/F#   G   A/C#   D/F#   G
And I'll never know   how much it cost to see   my sin   upon   that cross

     A/C#   D/F#   G   A/C#   D/F#   G   A7sus
And I'll never know   how much it cost to see   my sin   upon   that cross

(REPEAT CHORUS)

© 2000 Kingsway's Thankyou Music. All rights in the Western Hemisphere administered by EMI Christian Music Publishing.
P.O. Box 5085, Brentwood, TN 37204-5085. All rights reserved. Used by permission.

Madly
STEVE FEE

Capo 2 (E)

CHORUS 1:

     A/E   E   A/E   E
And I'm madly in love with You, and I'm madly in love with You
     A/E   E   A/E   E
And I'm madly in love with You, and I'm madly in love with You

SECTION 1:

       C#m B   A   E
Let what we do in here, fill the streets out there
    A   E   B   E
Let us dance for You, let us dance for You
       C#m B   A   E
Let what we do in here, fill the streets out there
    A   E   B   E (A2 E Bm7 E A2 E Bm7 E) *2nd time*
Let us dance for You, let us dance for You

(REPEAT CHORUS & SECTION 1)

SECTION 2:

        A   E
All of my life   and nothing less
      B   E
I offer to You   my righteousness
        A   E
All of my life   and nothing less
      B   E
I offer to You   my righteousness

CHORUS 2:

     A   E   Bsus   E
And I'm madly in love with You, and I'm madly in love with You
     A   E   Bsus   E
And I'm madly in love with You, and I'm madly in love with You

(REPEAT CHORUS 1)

© 2002 worshiptogether.com songs / Six Steps Music. Administered by EMI Christian Music Publishing.
P.O. Box 5085, Brentwood, TN 37204-5085. All rights reserved. Used by permission.

My Glorious

STUART GARRARD and MARTIN SMITH

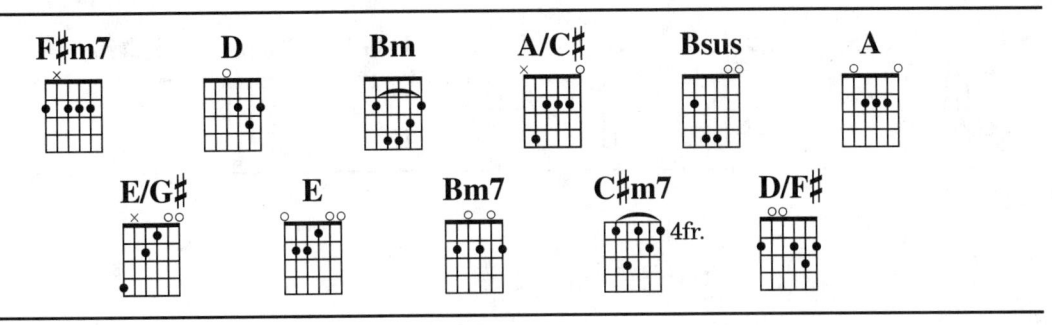

VERSE 1:

F#m7   D   Bm
The world's shaking with the love of God

F#m7   D   Bm
Great and glorious, let the whole earth sing

      D   A/C#
And all you ever do is change the old for new

Bsus
People we believe that

CHORUS:

A   E/G#   F#m7   E
God is bigger than the air I breathe, the world we'll leave

A   E/G#   F#m7   E   (F#m7 Bm7 C#m7) *1st time*
God will save the day, and all will say my glorious!

VERSE 2:

F#m7   D   Bm
Clouds are breaking, heaven's come to earth

F#m7   D   Bm
Hearts awak'ning, let the church bells ring

      D   A/C#
And all you ever do is change the old for new

Bsus
People we believe that

(REPEAT CHORUS)

TAG:

      D   E   D/F#   E
My glorious, my glorious, my glorious, my glorious

      D   E   D/F#   E/G#   A
My glorious, my glorious, my glorious, my glorious

© 2000 Curious? Music UK. All rights in the US and Canada administered by EMI Christian Music Publishing.
P.O. Box 5085, Brentwood, TN 37204-5085. All rights reserved. Used by permission.

Our Love Is Loud

DAVID CROWDER

Chords: E F#m7 C#m7 A2 E/D# E/G# Bsus D2

Capo 1 (G)

VERSE 1:

```
            E    F#m7         C#m7    A2
When we sing,     hear our songs    to You
            E    F#m7         C#m7    A2
When we dance,    feel us move    to You
            E    F#m7         C#m7    A2
When we laugh,    fill our smiles    with You
            E       F#m7      C#m7          A2
When we lift   our voices louder still, can    You hear us? Can    You feel?
```

CHORUS:

```
       E           E/D#           C#m7  A2
We love   You, Lord, we love    You, we love You
       E           E/D#           C#m7  A2  (E  E/D#  C#m7  A2)  1st time
We love   You, Lord, we love    You, we love You
```

VERSE 2:

```
            E      F#m7         C#m7    A2
When we sing   loud,     hear our songs    to You
              E      F#m7         C#m7    A2
When we dance  'round,    feel us move    to You
            E       F#m7         C#m7    A2
When we laugh   aloud,    fill our smiles    with You
            E       F#m7      C#m7          A2
When we lift   our voices louder still, can    You hear us? Can    You feel?
```

(REPEAT CHORUS)

BRIDGE:

```
          E           F#m7        E/G#                  A2
And our love   is big, our love    is loud. Fill    this place with this    love, now
          E           F#m7        E/G#                  A2
And our love   is big, our love    is loud. Fill    this place with this    love, now
              Bsus         C#m7              D2
And our love is big, our love    is loud. Fill    this place with this    love, now
      A2         Bsus        C#m7              D2
And our love   is big, our love    is loud. Fill    this place with this    love, now
```

© 2002 worshiptogether.com songs / Six Steps Music. Administered by EMI Christian Music Publishing.
P.O. Box 5085, Brentwood, TN 37204-5085. All rights reserved. Used by permission.

(REPEAT CHORUS)

TAG:

     E   E/D#
We lift   our voices louder still

       C#m7   A2
Our God   is near, our God   is here

     E   E/D#
We lift   our voices louder still

       C#m7   A2   E
Our God   is near, our God   is here

Prepare the Way

CHARLIE HALL and LOUIE GIGLIO

D   Bm   D/F#   G2

CHORUS:

```
  D              Bm              D/F#                      G2
  Prepare the way,   prepare the way,    prepare the way of the Lord
  D              Bm              D/F#                      G2
  Prepare the way,   prepare the way,    prepare the way of the Lord
  D   Bm   D/F#   G2
Jesus, Jesus, Jesus, Jesus
  D   Bm   D/F#   G2
Jesus, Jesus, Jesus, Jesus
```

VERSE 1:

```
  D                       Bm
  You are the Light of the world,    You are the Light of the world
D/F#                          G2
  You are the Light of the world, Jesus
  D                       Bm
  You are the Light of the world,    You are the Light of the world
D/F#                          G2
  You are the Light of the world, Jesus
```

VERSE 2:

```
  D                       Bm
  You are the King of the earth,    You are the King of the earth
D/F#                          G2
  You are the King of the earth, Jesus.
  D                       Bm
  You are the King of the earth,    You are the King of the earth
D/F#                          G2
  You are the King of the earth, Jesus.
```

BRIDGE:

```
       D              Bm            D/F#                G2
Jesus, Jesus, Jesus, Jesus, Jesus,   Jesus, Jesus
       D              Bm            D/F#                G2
Jesus, Jesus, Jesus, Jesus, Jesus,   Jesus, Jesus
```

(REPEAT CHORUS)

© 2002 worshiptogether.com songs / Six Steps Music. Administered by EMI Christian Music Publishing.
P.O. Box 5085, Brentwood, TN 37204-5085. All rights reserved. Used by permission.

Psalm 126
CHARLIE HALL

| D | A7sus/E | D/F# | G2 | Asus | A | D/C | B♭maj7 | Gm7 |

SECTION 1:

D   A7sus/E
  When the Lord brought back the captive ones   of Zion

D   A7sus/E
  We were like those who dreamed

D   A7sus/E
  Our mouths are filled with laughter,   our tongue with joyful shouting

D   A7sus/E   D/F# G2 Asus
  They say among the nations, the   Lord   has done great things for them

                                    D/F#   G2 Asus
Oh, the Lord has done great things   for us

                                    D/F#   G2 Asus
Oh, the Lord has done great things   for us

                     D/F# G2   Asus
We are filled with joy,   we are filled with joy

SECTION 2:

    D   A   A7sus/E
You have done great things,

    D   A   A7sus/E
You have done great things,

        D   A   A7sus/E
Yeah, You have done great things,   Father

    D   A   A7sus/E
You have done great things,

(REPEAT SECTIONS 1 & 2)

SECTION 3:

               D   D/C
You've restored   our hearts; like streams,   they flow

  B♭maj7   Gm7
Those   who sowed in tears have reaped   their joy

D   D/C   B♭maj7   (Asus) *2nd time*
  And return with shouts   and songs, carrying   the fruit of God

(REPEAT SECTION 3)

(REPEAT SECTION 2)

© 2002 worshiptogether.com songs / Six Steps Music. Administered by EMI Christian Music Publishing.
P.O. Box 5085, Brentwood, TN 37204-5085. All rights reserved. Used by permission.

Savior of the World
CHARLIE HALL

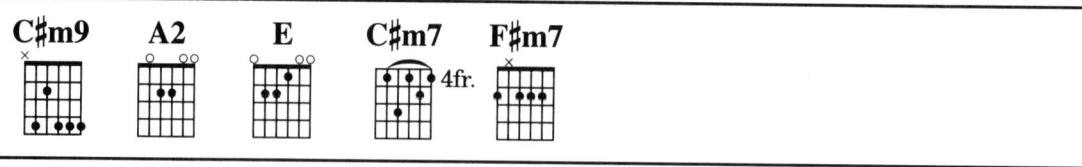

C#m9   A2   E   C#m7   F#m7

VERSE 1:

C#m9 A2   C#m9 A2
   There's a song   that the lost one sings
C#m9 A2   C#m9   A2
   When they are found and move   from dark   into the light
C#m9 A2   C#m9 A2
   There's a song   that the child redeemed
C#m9 A2   C#m9   A2   C#m9 A2 C#m9 A2
   Will sing out loud, and they   will run into the Father's arms

CHORUS:

          E
They sing: Oh Jesus, lifted up on high
C#m9
   Crucified for fallen man
A2
   You died and then You rose again
       F#m7
Oh Jesus, Savior of the world
E
   You've beaten death, and given life
C#m7
   You came to set the prisoner free
A2
   You died 'cause You're in love with me
       F#m7   (E) *Last time*
Oh Jesus, Savior of the world

© 1998 worshiptogether.com songs / Six Steps Music. Administered by EMI Christian Music Publishing.
P.O. Box 5085, Brentwood, TN 37204-5085. All rights reserved. Used by permission.

Sweep Me Away

CHARLIE HALL, KENDALL COMBS, WILL HUNT, BRIAN BERGMAN and TODD CROMWELL

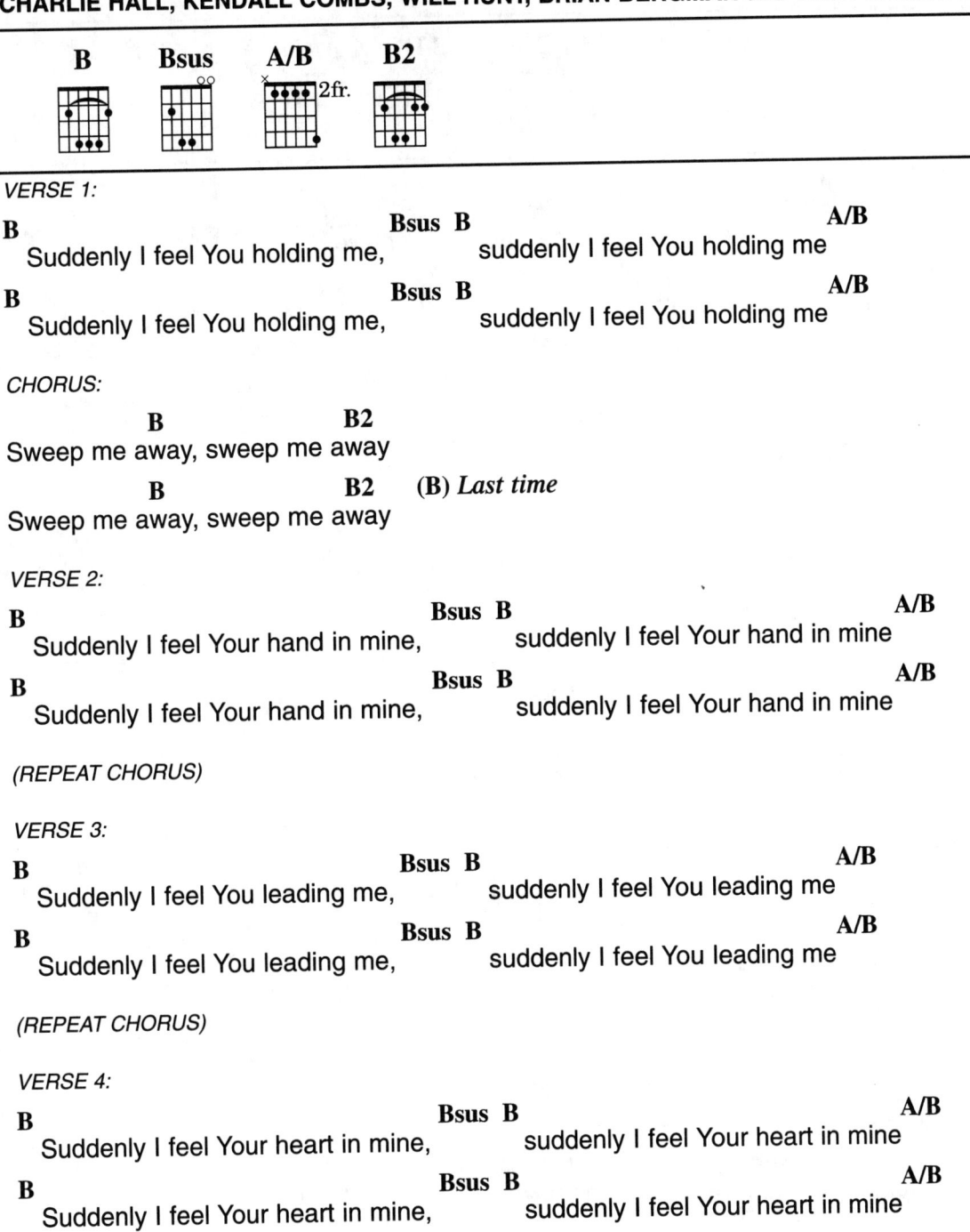

B   Bsus   A/B   B2

VERSE 1:

B   Bsus   B   A/B
  Suddenly I feel You holding me,   suddenly I feel You holding me

B   Bsus   B   A/B
  Suddenly I feel You holding me,   suddenly I feel You holding me

CHORUS:

        B   B2
Sweep me away, sweep me away

        B   B2   (B) *Last time*
Sweep me away, sweep me away

VERSE 2:

B   Bsus   B   A/B
  Suddenly I feel Your hand in mine,   suddenly I feel Your hand in mine

B   Bsus   B   A/B
  Suddenly I feel Your hand in mine,   suddenly I feel Your hand in mine

(REPEAT CHORUS)

VERSE 3:

B   Bsus   B   A/B
  Suddenly I feel You leading me,   suddenly I feel You leading me

B   Bsus   B   A/B
  Suddenly I feel You leading me,   suddenly I feel You leading me

(REPEAT CHORUS)

VERSE 4:

B   Bsus   B   A/B
  Suddenly I feel Your heart in mine,   suddenly I feel Your heart in mine

B   Bsus   B   A/B
  Suddenly I feel Your heart in mine,   suddenly I feel Your heart in mine

(REPEAT CHORUS)

© 2002 worshiptogether.com songs / Six Steps Music. Administered by EMI Christian Music Publishing.
P.O. Box 5085, Brentwood, TN 37204-5085. All rights reserved. Used by permission.

Wonderful King

DAVID CROWDER

E   E/G#   A2   F#m7   Bsus   B/D#   A/C#

SECTION 1:

E   E/G#   A2   E   E/G#   A2
We are here   because of grace, because of love

E   E/G#   A2   E   E/G#   A2
We are here   because of You, because of You

E   E/G#   A2   E   E/G#   A2
You are here   because of grace, because of love

E   E/G#   A2   E   E/G#   A2
And You are here   because of You, because of You

SECTION 2:

F#m7   E/G#   A2   E/G#   F#m7   E/G#
You fill our hearts with more than we can hold inside

A2   E/G#   F#m7   E/G#   A2
And so we sing

E   E/G# A2   E   E/G# A2
Beautiful Savior, wonderful King

E   E/G# A2   E   E/G# A2
Beautiful Savior, wonderful King

(LAST HALF SECTION 1)

E   E/G#   A2   E   E/G#   A2
You are here   because of grace, because of love

E   E/G#   A2   E   E/G#   A2
And we are here   because of You, because of You

(REPEAT SECTION 2)

SECTION 4:

F#m7   E/G#   A2
Oh, beautiful sound, the joy of heaven here

Bsus   A/C#
Oh, wonderful sound, love our heaven now

B/D#   A2
Oh, beautiful sound, the joy of heaven here

Bsus
Oh, wonderful sound, love our heaven now

E   E/G# A2   E   E/G# A2
Beautiful Savior, wonderful King

E   E/G# A2   E   E/G# A2
Beautiful Savior, wonderful King

© 2002 worshiptogether.com songs / Six Steps Music. Administered by EMI Christian Music Publishing.
P.O. Box 5085, Brentwood, TN 37204-5085. All rights reserved. Used by permission.

Come, Thou Fount of Every Blessing

Traditional; Arr. by DAVID CROWDER

Come, Thou Fount of ev'ry blessing
Tune my heart to sing Thy grace
Streams of mercy, never ceasing
Call for songs of loudest praise
Teach me some melodious sonnet
Sung by flaming tongues above
Praise the mount; I'm fixed upon it
Mount of God's redeeming love

Here I raise my Ebeneezer
Hither to Thy help I'm come
And I hope by Thy good pleasure
Safely to arrive at home.
Jesus sought me when a stranger
Wand'ring from the fold of God
He, to rescue me from danger
Interposed His precious blood

O to grace how great a debtor
Daily I'm constrained to be!
Let Thy goodness, like a fetter
Bind my wand'ring heart to Thee
Prone to wander, Lord, I feel it
Prone to leave the God I love
Here's my heart, O take and seal it
Seal it for Thy courts above

Arrangement © 2002 worshiptogether.com songs / Six Steps Music. Administered by EMI Christian Music Publishing. P.O. Box 5085, Brentwood, TN 37204-5085. All rights reserved. Used by permission.

Dance in the River
MARTIN SMITH

We're gonna dance in the river, yeah
We're gonna dance in the river, yeah
We're gonna dance in the river, yeah
We're gonna dance in the river, yeah

We're gonna dance in the river, yeah
We're gonna dance in the river, yeah
We're gonna dance in the river, yeah
We're gonna dance in the river, yeah

© 2002 Curious? Music UK. All rights in the US and Canada administered by EMI Christian Music Publishing.
P.O. Box 5085, Brentwood, TN 37204-5085. All rights reserved. Used by permission.

Enough
CHRIS TOMLIN and LOUIE GIGLIO

All of You is more than enough
For all of me, for ev'ry thirst
And ev'ry need. You satisfy
Me with Your love, and all I have in You
Is more than enough

You're my supply, my breath of life
Still more awesome than I know
You're my reward, worth living for
Still more awesome than I know

You're my sacrifice of greatest price
Still more awesome than I know
You're my coming King, You are ev'rything
Still more awesome than I know

More than all I want
More than all I need, yeah
You are more than enough for me
More than all I know
More than all I can see
You are more than enough

© 2002 worshiptogether.com songs / Six Steps Music. Administered by EMI Christian Music Publishing.
P.O. Box 5085, Brentwood, TN 37204-5085. All rights reserved. Used by permission.

Famous One
CHRIS TOMLIN and JESSE REEVES

You are the Lord
The famous One, famous One
Great is Your name in all the earth
The heavens declare
You're glorious, glorious
Great is Your fame beyond the earth

And for all You've done and yet to do
With ev'ry breath, I'm praising You
Desire of nations and ev'ry heart
You alone are God
You alone are God

The Morning Star is shining through
And ev'ry eye is watching You
Reveal Thy nature and miracles
You are beautiful
You are beautiful

© 2002 worshiptogether.com songs / Six Steps Music. Administered by EMI Christian Music Publishing.
P.O. Box 5085, Brentwood, TN 37204-5085. All rights reserved. Used by permission.

Forever
CHRIS TOMLIN

Give thanks to the Lord our God and King
His love endures forever
For He is good, He is above all things
His love endures forever
Sing praise, sing praise

With a mighty hand and outstretched arm
His love endures forever
For the life that's been reborn
His love endures forever
Sing praise, sing praise
Sing praise, sing praise

Forever God is faithful, forever God is strong
Forever God is with us, forever, forever

From the rising to the setting sun
His love endures forever
And by the grace of God we will carry on
His love endures forever
Sing praise, sing praise
Sing praise, sing praise

© 2001 worshiptogether.com songs / Six Steps Music. Administered by EMI Christian Music Publishing.
P.O. Box 5085, Brentwood, TN 37204-5085. All rights reserved. Used by permission.

God of Wonders
MARC BYRD and STEVE HINDALONG

Lord of all creation
Of water, earth and sky
The heavens are Your tabernacle
Glory to the Lord on high

God of wonders beyond our galaxy
You are holy, holy; the universe declares
   Your majesty
You are holy, holy; Lord of heaven and earth
Lord of heaven and earth

Early in the morning
I will celebrate the light
And as I stumble in the darkness
I will call Your name by night

Hallelujah! to the Lord of heaven and earth
Hallelujah! to the Lord of heaven and earth
Hallelujah! to the Lord of heaven and earth

© 2000 Storm Boy Music / New Spring Publishing / Never Say Never Songs.
All rights reserved. Used by permission.

God of Wrath
DAVID CROWDER

God of wrath, God of love
God of earth and God above
God of hope, God of peace
God of you and God of me

God of day, God of night
God the just and God the light
God of the strong, God of the weak
God of you and God of me

My love for You, my heart for You
My life for You, all I am for You
My love for You, my heart for You
My life for You, all I am for You

Blood through my veins for You
I give my world to You
All I am and all I have
I lay it down for You
Dancing 'round with You
Spinning 'round with You
Laughing loud with You
My love, my love

© 2002 worshiptogether.com songs / Six Steps Music. Administered by EMI Christian Music Publishing.
P.O. Box 5085, Brentwood, TN 37204-5085. All rights reserved. Used by permission.

Here I Am to Worship
TIM HUGHES

Light of the World
You stepped down into darkness,
Opened my eyes, let me see
Beauty that made this heart adore You
Hope of a life spent with You

So here I am to worship
Here I am to bow down
Here I am to say that You're my God
And You're altogether lovely
Altogether worthy
Altogether wonderful to me

King of all days, oh so highly exalted
Glorious in heaven above
Humbly You came to the Earth You created
All for love's sake became poor

And I'll never know how much it cost
To see my sin upon that cross
And I'll never know how much it cost
To see my sin upon that cross

© 2000 Kingsway's Thankyou Music. All rights in the Western Hemisphere administered by EMI Christian Music Publishing. P.O. Box 5085, Brentwood, TN 37204-5085. All rights reserved. Used by permission.

Madly
STEVE FEE

And I'm madly in love with You
And I'm madly in love with You
And I'm madly in love with You
And I'm madly in love with You

Let what we do in here
Fill the streets out there.
Let us dance for You
Let us dance for You
Let what we do in here
Fill the streets out there
Let us dance for You
Let us dance for You

All of my life and nothing less
I offer to You my righteousness
Yeah, all of my life and nothing less
I offer to You my righteousness

© 2002 worshiptogether.com songs / Six Steps Music. Administered by EMI Christian Music Publishing.
P.O. Box 5085, Brentwood, TN 37204-5085. All rights reserved. Used by permission.

My Glorious
STUART GARRARD and MARTIN SMITH

The world's shaking with the love of God
Great and glorious, let the whole earth sing
And all you ever do is change the old for new
People we believe that

God is bigger than the air I breathe
The world we'll leave.
God will save the day
And all will say my glorious!

Clouds are breaking, heaven's come to earth
Hearts awak'ning, let the church bells ring
And all you ever do is change the old for new
People we believe that

My glorious, my glorious
My glorious, my glorious
My glorious, my glorious
My glorious, my glorious

© 2000 Curious? Music UK. All rights in the US and Canada administered by EMI Christian Music Publishing.
P.O. Box 5085, Brentwood, TN 37204-5085. All rights reserved. Used by permission.

Our Love Is Loud
DAVID CROWDER

When we sing, hear our songs to You
When we dance, feel us move to You
When we laugh, fill our smiles with You
When we lift our voices louder still, can You hear us?
Can You feel?

We love You, Lord, we love You, we love You
We love You, Lord, we love You, we love You

When we sing loud, hear our songs to You
When we dance 'round, feel us move to You
When we laugh aloud, fill our smiles with You
When we lift our voices louder still, can You hear us?
Can You feel?

And our love is big, our love is loud
Fill this place with this love, now
And our love is big, our love is loud
Fill this place with this love, now
And our love is big, our love is loud
Fill this place with this love, now
And our love is big, our love is loud
Fill this place with this love, now

We lift our voices louder still
Our God is near, our God is here
We lift our voices louder still
Our God is near, our God is here

© 2002 worshiptogether.com songs / Six Steps Music. Administered by EMI Christian Music Publishing.
P.O. Box 5085, Brentwood, TN 37204-5085. All rights reserved. Used by permission.

Prepare the Way
CHARLIE HALL and LOUIE GIGLIO

Prepare the way, prepare the way
Prepare the way of the Lord
Prepare the way, prepare the way
Prepare the way of the Lord
Jesus, Jesus, Jesus, Jesus
Jesus, Jesus, Jesus, Jesus

You are the Light of the world
You are the Light of the world
You are the Light of the world, Jesus
You are the Light of the world
You are the Light of the world
You are the Light of the world, Jesus

You are the King of the earth
You are the King of the earth
You are the King of the earth, Jesus.
You are the King of the earth
You are the King of the earth
You are the King of the earth, Jesus.

Jesus, Jesus, Jesus, Jesus
Jesus, Jesus, Jesus
Jesus, Jesus, Jesus, Jesus
Jesus, Jesus, Jesus

© 2002 worshiptogether.com songs / Six Steps Music. Administered by EMI Christian Music Publishing.
P.O. Box 5085, Brentwood, TN 37204-5085. All rights reserved. Used by permission.

Psalm 126
CHARLIE HALL

When the Lord brought back
The captive ones of Zion
We were like those who dreamed
Our mouths are filled with laughter
Our tongue with joyful shouting
They say among the nations
The Lord has done great things for them
Oh, the Lord has done great things for us
Oh, the Lord has done great things for us
We are filled with joy, we are filled with joy

You have done great things
You have done great things
Yeah, You have done great things, Father
You have done great things

You've restored our hearts
Like streams, they flow
Those who sowed in tears
Have reaped their joy
And return with shouts and songs
Carrying the fruit of God

© 2002 worshiptogether.com songs / Six Steps Music. Administered by EMI Christian Music Publishing.
P.O. Box 5085, Brentwood, TN 37204-5085. All rights reserved. Used by permission.

Savior of the World
CHARLIE HALL

There's a song that the lost one sings
When they are found and move from dark into the light
There's a song that the child redeemed
Will sing out loud, and they will run into the Father's arms

They sing: Oh Jesus, lifted up on high
Crucified for fallen man
You died and then You rose again
Oh Jesus, Savior of the world
You've beaten death, and given life
You came to set the prisoner free
You died 'cause You're in love with me
Oh Jesus, Savior of the world

© 1998 worshiptogether.com songs / Six Steps Music. Administered by EMI Christian Music Publishing.
P.O. Box 5085, Brentwood, TN 37204-5085. All rights reserved. Used by permission.

Sweep Me Away

*Charlie Hall, Kendall Combs, Will Hunt, Brian Bergman
and Todd Cromwell*

Suddenly I feel You holding me
Suddenly I feel You holding me
Suddenly I feel You holding me
Suddenly I feel You holding me

Sweep me away, sweep me away
Sweep me away, sweep me away

Suddenly I feel Your hand in mine
Suddenly I feel Your hand in mine
Suddenly I feel Your hand in mine
Suddenly I feel Your hand in mine

Suddenly I feel You leading me
Suddenly I feel You leading me
Suddenly I feel You leading me
Suddenly I feel You leading me

Suddenly I feel Your heart in mine
Suddenly I feel Your heart in mine
Suddenly I feel Your heart in mine
Suddenly I feel Your heart in mine

© 2002 worshiptogether.com songs / Six Steps Music. Administered by EMI Christian Music Publishing.
P.O. Box 5085, Brentwood, TN 37204-5085. All rights reserved. Used by permission.

Wonderful King
DAVID CROWDER

We are here because of grace
Because of love
We are here because of You
Because of You
You are here because of grace
Because of love
And You are here because of You
Because of You

You fill our hearts with more than we can
　hold inside
And so we sing
Beautiful Savior, wonderful King
Beautiful Savior, wonderful King

You are here because of grace
Because of love
And we are here because of You
Because of You

Oh, beautiful sound, the joy of heaven here
Oh, wonderful sound, love our heaven now
Oh, beautiful sound, the joy of heaven here
Oh, wonderful sound, love our heaven now

Beautiful Savior, wonderful King
Beautiful Savior, wonderful King

© 2002 worshiptogether.com songs / Six Steps Music. Administered by EMI Christian Music Publishing.
P.O. Box 5085, Brentwood, TN 37204-5085. All rights reserved. Used by permission.